SCHOLASTIC INC.

NEW YORK   TORONTO   LONDON   AUCKLAND

SYDNEY   MEXICO CITY   NEW DELHI   HONG KONG

ISBN 978-0-545-17765-8

LEGO, the LEGO logo, the Brick and the Knob configurations and Minifigure are trademarks of the LEGO Group.
©2010 The LEGO Group. Produced by Scholastic Inc. under license from the LEGO Group.

All rights reserved. Published by Scholastic Inc.

SCHOLASTIC and associated logos are trademarks and/or registered trademarks of Scholastic Inc.

12 13 14 15/0

20 40

Printed in the U.S.A.
First printing, July 2010

"Let's get started," says the foreman to his crew. "First, we need to clear the construction site!"

One worker chips away at a large rock with a jackhammer. Other crewmembers use shovels and wheelbarrows to take away the rubble.

5

This job is going to take some big trucks! An excavator can dig out heavy boulders.

Once the rocks are out of the ground, the front-end loader scoops them up with its bucket. It drops the rocks into a heavy-duty dump truck. The truck will haul away the boulders.

7631

7630

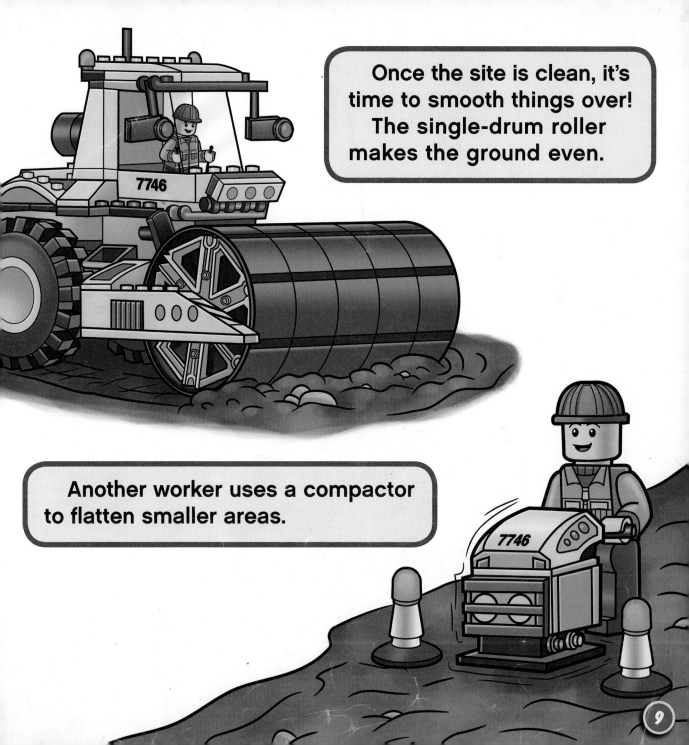

Once the site is clean, it's time to smooth things over! The single-drum roller makes the ground even.

Another worker uses a compactor to flatten smaller areas.

9

Every new building needs a strong foundation. The foreman talks to the crew. "Looking good," he says. "Now it's time to pour the concrete."

Here comes a worker with the concrete. The drum keeps the concrete mixing until it's ready to pour.

Some workers pour the concrete while others spread it with shovels. Then they make the surface smooth and even.

It will take a while for the concrete to dry.
But there's plenty of work to do in the meantime!
A huge delivery truck arrives loaded with
building supplies.

One worker uses a skid loader to haul supplies. It's perfect for smaller loads.

14

After a few days, the foundation is dry and hard. "Let's start building!" says the foreman.

Construction workers fasten metal struts to the foundation. This builds a sturdy frame for the walls, floors, and ceilings.

It's time for a bigger crane!
The mobile crane's long boom lifts large sections into place.

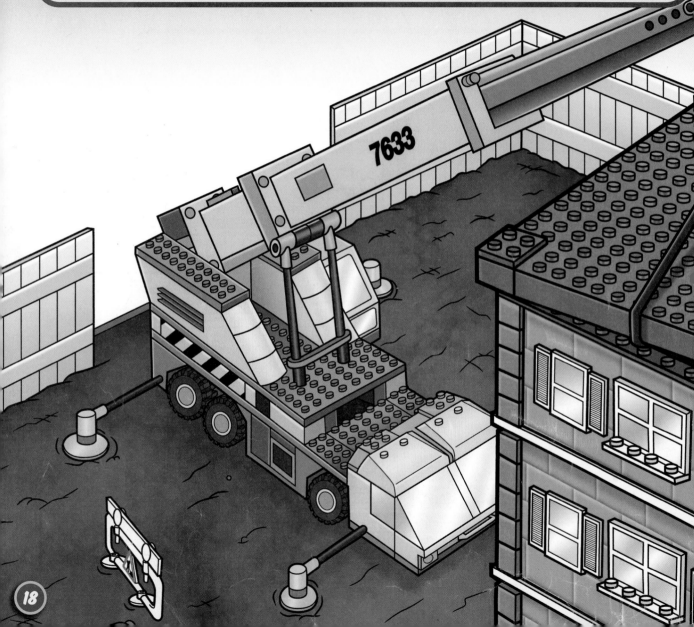

The foreman talks to the crane operator to get the floor section into just the right position. This building is really coming together!

19

Here is the biggest crane yet!

This tower crane has a very strong winch. A winch is a motor that winds the crane's thick cable. It pulls the load to the very top of the building.

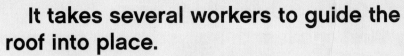

It takes several workers to guide the roof into place.

The foreman makes sure everything at the site goes smoothly.

23